ROBIN BROOKS is a freelance writer who lives in Cheltenham. His work includes plays for Radio 4, newspaper and magazine features, books, video-scripts and commercial copywriting. Robin writes regularly on local interest subjects for the *Gloucestershire Echo* and *Gloucester Citizen*.

FRANCIS FRITH'S
LIVING MEMORIES

GLOUCESTERSHIRE
LIVING MEMORIES

ROBIN BROOKS

THE FRANCIS
FRITH
COLLECTION

First published in the United Kingdom in 2004 by
Frith Book Company Ltd

Hardback Edition 2005
ISBN 1-85937-642-8

British Library Cataloguing in Publication Data

Gloucestershire Living Memories
Robin Brooks

Frith Book Company Ltd
Frith's Barn, Teffont,
Salisbury, Wiltshire SP3 5QP
Tel: +44 (0) 1722 716 376
Email: info@francisfrith.co.uk
www.francisfrith.co.uk

Printed and bound in Great Britain

Front Cover: **CIRENCESTER,** *Cricklade Street c1955* C106052
Frontispiece: **BROCKWEIR,** *c1965* B533014

*The colour-tinting is for illustrative purposes only, and is not intended to be
historically accurate*

AS WITH ANY HISTORICAL DATABASE THE FRITH ARCHIVE IS CONSTANTLY
BEING CORRECTED AND IMPROVED, AND THE PUBLISHERS WOULD
WELCOME INFORMATION ON OMISSIONS OR INACCURACIES

CONTENTS

FRANCIS FRITH
VICTORIAN PIONEER

FRANCIS FRITH, founder of the world-famous photographic archive, was a complex and multi-talented man. A devout Quaker and a highly successful Victorian businessman, he was philosophic by nature and pioneering in outlook.

By 1855 he had already established a wholesale grocery business in Liverpool, and sold it for the astonishing sum of £200,000, which is the equivalent today of over £15,000,000. Now a very rich man, he was able to indulge his passion for travel. As a child he had pored over travel books written by early explorers, and his fancy and imagination had been stirred by family holidays to the sublime mountain regions of Wales and Scotland. 'What lands of spirit-stirring and enriching scenes and places!' he had written. He was to return to these scenes of grandeur in later years to 'recapture the thousands of vivid and tender memories', but with a different purpose. Now in his thirties, and captivated by the new science of photography, Frith set out on a series of pioneering journeys up the Nile and to the Near East that occupied him from 1856 unti 1860.

INTRIGUE AND EXPLORATION

These far-flung journeys were packed with intrigue and adventure. In his life story, written when he was sixty-three, Frith tells of being held captive by bandits, and of fighting 'an awful midnight battle to the very point of surrender with a deadly pack of hungry, wild dogs'. Wearing flowing Arab costume, Frith arrived at Akaba by camel seventy years before Lawrence of Arabia, where he encountered 'desert princes and rival sheikhs, blazing with jewel-hilted swords'.

He was the first photographer to venture beyond the sixth cataract of the Nile. Africa was still the mysterious 'Dark Continent', and Stanley and Livingstone's historic meeting was a decade into the future. The conditions for picture taking confound belief. He laboured for hours in his wicker dark-room in the sweltering heat of the desert, while the volatile chemicals fizzed dangerously in their trays. Back in London he exhibited his photographs and was 'rapturously cheered' by members of the Royal Society. His reputation as a photographer was made overnight.

VENTURE OF A LIFE-TIME

Characteristically, Frith quickly spotted the opportunity to create a new business as a specialist publisher of photographs. He lived in an era of immense and sometimes violent change. For the poor in the early part of Victoria's reign work was exhausting and the hours long, and people had precious little free time to enjoy themselves. Most people had no transport other than a cart or gig at their disposal, and rarely

travelled far beyond the boundaries of their own town or village. However, by the 1870s the railways had threaded their way across the country, and Bank Holidays and half-day Saturdays had been made obligatory by Act of Parliament. All of a sudden the working man and his family were able to enjoy days out and see a little more of the world.

With typical business acumen, Francis Frith foresaw that these new tourists would enjoy having souvenirs to commemorate their days out. In 1860 he married Mary Ann Rosling and set out on a new career: his aim was to photograph every city, town and village in Britain. For the next thirty years he travelled the country by train and by pony and trap, producing fine photographs of seaside resorts and beauty spots that were keenly bought by millions of Victorians. These prints were painstakingly pasted into family albums and pored over during the dark nights of winter, rekindling precious memories of summer excursions.

THE RISE OF FRITH & CO

Frith's studio was soon supplying retail shops all over the country. To meet the demand he gathered about him a small team of photographers, and published the work of independent artist-photographers of the calibre of Roger Fenton and Francis Bedford. In order to gain some understanding of the scale of Frith's business one only has to look at the catalogue issued by Frith & Co in 1886: it runs to some 670 pages, listing not only many thousands of views of the British Isles but also many photographs of most European countries, and China, Japan, the USA and Canada - note the sample page shown on page 9 from the hand-written Frith & Co ledgers recording the pictures. By 1890 Frith had created the greatest specialist photographic publishing company in the world, with over 2,000 sales outlets - more than the combined number that Boots and WH Smith have today! The picture on the nest page shows the Frith & Co display board at Ingleton in the Yorkshire Dales (left of window). Beautifully constructed with a mahogany frame and gilt inserts, it could display up to a dozen local scenes.

POSTCARD BONANZA

The ever-popular holiday postcard we know today took many years to develop. In 1870 the Post Office issued the first plain cards, with a pre-printed stamp on one face. In 1894 they allowed other publishers' cards to be sent through the mail with an attached adhesive halfpenny stamp. Demand grew rapidly, and in 1895 a new size of postcard was permitted called the court card, but there was little room for illustration. In 1899, a year after Frith's death, a new card measuring 5.5 x 3.5 inches became the standard format, but it was not until 1902 that the divided back came into being, so that the address and message could be on one face and a full-size illustration on the other. Frith & Co were in the vanguard of postcard development: Frith's sons Eustace and Cyril continued their father's monumental task, expanding the number of views offered to the public and recording more and more places in Britain, as the coasts and countryside were opened up to mass travel.

Francis Frith had died in 1898 at his villa in Cannes, his great project still growing. The archive he created continued in business for another seventy years. By 1970 it contained over a third of a million pictures showing 7,000 British towns and villages.

FRANCIS FRITH'S LEGACY

Frith's legacy to us today is of immense significance and value, for the magnificent archive of evocative photographs he created provides a unique record of change in the cities, towns and villages throughout Britain over a century and more. Frith and his fellow studio photographers revisited locations many times down the years to update their views, compiling for us an enthralling and colourful pageant of British life and character.

We are fortunate that Frith was dedicated to recording the minutiae of everyday life. For it is this sheer wealth of visual data, the painstaking chronicle of changes in dress, transport, street layouts, buildings, housing, engineering and landscape that captivates us so much today. His remarkable images offer us a powerful link with the past and with the lives of our ancestors.

THE VALUE OF THE ARCHIVE TODAY

Computers have now made it possible for Frith's many thousands of images to be accessed almost instantly. Frith's images are increasingly used as visual resources, by social historians, by researchers into genealogy and ancestry, by architects and town planners, and by teachers involved in local history projects.

In addition, the archive offers every one of us an opportunity to examine the places where we and our families have lived and worked down the years. Highly successful in Frith's own era, the archive is now, a century and more on, entering a new phase of popularity. Historians consider the Francis Frith Collection to be of prime national importance. It is the only archive of its kind remaining in private ownership. Francis Frith's archive is now housed in an historic timber barn in the beautiful village of Teffont in Wiltshire. Its founder would not recognize the archive office as it is today. In place of the many thousands of dusty boxes containing glass plate negatives and an all-pervading odour of photographic chemicals, there are now ranks of computer screens. He would be amazed to watch his images travelling round the world at unimaginable speeds through internet lines.

The archive's future is both bright and exciting. Francis Frith, with his unshakeable belief in making photographs available to the greatest number of people, would undoubtedly approve of what is being done today with his lifetime's work. His photographs depicting our shared past are now bringing pleasure and enlightenment to millions around the world a century and more after his death.

GLOUCESTERSHIRE
AN INTRODUCTION

'As sure as God's in Gloucestershire' is a saying that has now largely fallen from use, but it serves as a reminder that the county is particularly blessed with fine ecclesiastical buildings. Tewkesbury's abbey, which was consecrated in 1121, vies with Gloucester cathedral in size and magnificence. At the Dissolution of the Monasteries, the townspeople of Tewkesbury paid £453 to buy the abbey from Henry VIII, which was said to be the value of the lead on the roof and the iron in the bells.

First-time visitors to the Cotswolds can be forgiven for puzzling over why so many great and splendid churches are often found in small and modest village settings. These are the 'Cotswold cathedrals', not really cathedrals at all, but parish churches that were funded by local merchants who became fabulously wealthy in the wool trade. In addition to the magnificent churches we see today, Gloucestershire was once home to monastic foundations, vast in scale and powerful

NORTHLEACH, *The Green c1955* N125008

10

in influence. Many of these buildings, such as those at Cirencester, Winchcombe and Hailes, were razed to ruin at the time of the Dissolution, and today just a few scattered stones remain to hint at the grandeur that once was.

If we delve even further back into history, we find that in Roman Britain Cirencester (Corinium) was second only in importance to London. The Corinium Museum in Park Street houses one of the finest collections of Roman artifacts in the country - the majority were found in and around the town - and attracts 75,000 visitors a year. Cirencester's role as a market centre was founded over 2,000 years ago, and continues to this day. Many other Cotswold towns also host ancient markets. Stow on the Wold, Chipping Campden ('Chipping' is derived from the Anglo-Saxon word for 'market') and others grew wealthy as market centres for the woollen industry, so fine market halls - sometimes raised on stone columns - are another characteristic feature of the rolling upland Cotswolds. An attractive example is the market hall at Tetbury, a town that possesses one of the greatest concentrations of buildings listed for their architectural importance in the country.

Stone is the traditional building material in the Cotswolds, in particular the honey-coloured limestone extracted from numerous small-scale quarries. This means that the towns and villages hereabouts blend comfortably into the landscape, because they are built from the ground on which they stand. Painswick's buildings, for example, are of stone taken from the nearby Beacon. If we are to credit human craft for lending so distinct a profile to the Cotswolds in the east and north of the county, then the dramatic landscape to the south-west must be attributed to the hand of nature. Tucked between the Severn and Wye

rivers, the Forest of Dean presents some of the finest scenery in the country. The villages may be less pretty than their Cotswold neighbours, but the Forest is a place with a wealth of history and a sense of independence that is tangible in its ancient customs, lore and laws. Mining was at the heart of the Forest economy until the industry went into decline on a commercial scale in the 1960s. Even today, though, Freeminers exercise their rights to dig coal, iron ore and ochre from private pits, as they have done for generations beyond recall. Dean Heritage Centre at Soudley, near Cinderford, is a must for anyone studying the Foresters' way of life down through the centuries. There we can learn about the Freeminers and the ways of this region.

On the other side of the Severn, to the south of Gloucestershire, yet another face of the county is presented, as this passage from a 1947 guide book on the valley town of Stroud describes: 'This busy and very picturesque town is situated in a most charming portion of Gloucestershire, and the valley along to Brimscombe is dotted with thriving factories, so placed that they in no way hinder or obstruct the beauty of the landscape. Stroud is a progressive town and visitors will be delighted with its beautiful surroundings'. Many of Stroud's buildings hark back to the town's industrial past; it used to be a manufacturing centre for the wool industry, and the quality of its cloth was renowned. Some of the former mills, usually sited on the streams that powered the mill wheels, can still be seen, though today their function has changed.

The main centres of population in Gloucestershire are the county city of Gloucester and the town of Cheltenham. Although they are geographically close and virtually the same size in numbers of residents, the two are quite different in character. Gloucester has the gravitas befitting a city that has been an important crossing point on the Severn since time long gone, and has played a significant role in the drama of British history for more than two millennia. Cheltenham, on the other hand, would probably still be the single-street market town it used to be, had not its meteoric development as a fashionable spa been kick-started when George III and the royal household came to stay in the late 18th century.

Natural beauty, rich history, elegant towns and picture book villages: by whatever criteria we apply, Gloucestershire is glorious. Britain's longest river reaches maturity here as it mean- ders to meet the sea. Most of the Cotswolds, the UK's largest designated Area of Outstanding Natural Beauty, rests within the county boundary. Then to add further contrast there is the Royal Forest of Dean, which embraces over 100 square miles of ancient woodland.

What is particular about Gloucestershire is that it offers so much variation in landscape. Uplands such as Cleeve Common spread beyond the Cotswold escarpment. Slimbridge - home to the Wildfowl Trust - and other wetlands are found along the Severn. Between the two is the flat vale that is one of the richest farm and market gardening areas in the country, while further

LEIGH, *The Old Post Office c1955* L344007

south steep stream-cut valleys radiate like spokes from Stroud and Nailsworth, towns that once generated industrial wealth.

It is a landscape that writers and composers have long found an inspiration. For proof, turn the pages of Laurie Lee's classic autobiography *Cider with Rosie*, browse the verses of Robert Frost, Lascelles Abercrombie and their fellow Dymock poets, or listen to the pastoral suites of Edward Elgar, Gustav Holst and Ralph Vaughan Williams.

Although the population of Gloucestershire is under 600,000, its settlements range from rural to industrial, and many have a compelling story to tell. The county city has had the distinction of being England's most inland port since the time of Elizabeth I. Over the past few decades Gloucester docks have been rejuvenated, and now rate as a magnet for over one million visitors each year. Another major attraction is the city's magnificent cathedral. Besides a history that spans 1,300 years, this has the most complete example of mediaeval cloisters in Britain (incidentally, the cloisters provide the setting for Hogwarts in the Harry Potter films), along with the tomb of King Edward II. At the east end of the chancel is the Crecy window, the largest single expanse of medieval stained glass in England.

Today, besides its attractions for shopaholics in search of retail therapy, Cheltenham is also a cultural centre. The well-established literature and music festivals, each with a full programme of fringe events, enjoy national prominence, while the more recently introduced jazz and folk festivals attract top-grade artists from around the globe. The Promenade is Cheltenham's best-known street, which extends in a tree-lined, straight stretch for just over a quarter of a mile, bordered by broad pavements, with fine shops to one side, and buildings and grand gardens to the other. It was laid out properly in 1818 and lined with 44 chestnut trees. Cheltenham's reputation as a garden town stretches back a century, and in recent decades the town has gained an enviable record in the Britain in Bloom competition. Cheltenham's famed architectural unity is a happy legacy of its era as a fashionable spa. George III came to town in 1788 and prompted a building boom that lasted about 40 years, during which time the four great estates of Bayshill, Pittville, Lansdown and Montpellier were planned and built.

The collection of photographs awaiting us between these covers spans the last half century or so. It seems appropriate that our pictorial tour around Gloucestershire should begin with the county city, along with its suburbs that were once separate villages and satellite settlements. Cheltenham and its sphere come next, followed by the Cotswold country to the east and north of the county, the valleys and vales to the south and finally the Forest of Dean. Inevitably, these divisions will not suit every reader perfectly. The tiny hamlet of Leigh, for example, is included here in the Cheltenham section, though it is pretty much equidistant from Gloucester and Tewkesbury, so arguments for its inclusion in either of those sections could easily be supported. But never mind. What is important here is that the selection of images presents a pleasing pictorial record of how Gloucestershire was in the 1950s and 60s, and the changes that have shaped its continuing story. Enjoy the journey.

AROUND GLOUCESTER

GLOUCESTER, *Westgate Street c1950* G20006

St Michael's tower (right), which dates from the mid 15th century, is all that remains of the city centre church today. The rest was demolished in 1955. Westgate Street is now pedestrianised, though its higgledy-piggledy character of individual shops and businesses in a variety of building styles remains intact. On the left of the photograph is the entrance to St John's Lane, where the *Gloucester Citizen* has been published daily since 1876.

▶ **GLOUCESTER**
Baker's Clock c1960 G20057

One of Gloucester's best-known features is the ingenious clock that stands at first floor level above G A Baker & Sons in Southgate Street. The shop was established on this site in 1882, but it was razed to the ground and rebuilt in 1904, which was when the clock appeared. The *Gloucester Journal* of 26 November 1904 gave this description: 'On the front of the shop is a clock made by Niehus Brothers of Bristol. It has five striking jacks representing England (John Bull) sounding note 'A'; Ireland (Irish girl) note 'B'; Scotland (The Cock of the North) note 'D'; Wales (Welsh girl) note 'G' and Father Time to strike the hours on note 'D' an octave below the quarters. The clock has a Graham dead-beat escapement and is extremely accurate.'

▶ **GLOUCESTER**
Eastgate Street c1950
G20018

The Saracen's Head, with its ornate, wrought iron portico (right), was one of the city centre's leading hotels. Others included The Bell Hotel and The New County in Southgate Street and The Fleece in Westgate Street. Next door to The Saracen's Head is the Guildhall, opened in 1892 to house the city's administrators. Its civic duties came to an end in 1985 when the building was taken over by the Cheltenham & Gloucester Building Society. Directly opposite we see the impressive pediment of the Eastgate Market entrance, which in 1973 was dismantled, then rebuilt stone by stone 130ft to the east.

GLOUCESTER, *Northgate Street from the Cross c1950* G20007

Samuel Long (right) was a well-established fishmonger, so the bustle of people outside the shop suggests that something tasty was on special offer - elvers or lampreys locally caught in the Severn, perhaps? Further down Northgate Street is The New Inn, still in business today and one of the best-preserved medieval galleried inns in the country. The building in the distance topped by the large clock face was Bon Marche, Gloucester's leading department store.

◄ **GLOUCESTER**
Northgate Street look-
ing towards London
Road c1950 G20019

The elegant spire in the distance tops St Peter's Roman Catholic church, which in its original form dated from 1789. However, the present building, which was designed by Gilbert Blount, was consecrated in 1868. To the left is the junction with Worcester Street leading towards Tewkesbury and the Midlands. Gloucester was Glevum to the Romans, and the cruciform street plan on which they built the city is clearly in evidence to this day.

GLOUCESTER
Eastgate Street c1960
G20072

Before by-passes and motorways, Gloucester's location as a route centre meant that virtually all traffic from the south-west heading north, and all traffic from South Wales heading east (and vice versa) passed over Gloucester Cross. Policemen on point duty at the Cross worked 40 minutes on, then had 20 minutes off, and in 1928 the Daily Mail described the officer on this harrowing duty as 'the busiest man in England'. In April 1934 traffic lights were installed, and PC Mince reserved a place for himself in city history as the last bobby to perform a regular shift on point duty at the Cross. On the day this photograph was taken in 1960, the traffic lights must have been out of action.

CHURCHDOWN
The Bat and Ball c1950 C103004

In 1938 The Bat and Bull was built directly behind a pub called The Old Elm Inn, which was then demolished. At that time a plan was mooted to re-route the main Cheltenham-Gloucester Road through Churchdown past The Old Elm Inn. Its owners, Flowers Brewery, believing a smart new pub in the contemporary roadhouse style would attract plenty of passing custom, demolished the old and built the new. Villagers were sorry to see the old pub go - and no doubt the directors of Flowers Brewery were miffed when the A40 was not re-routed after all.

BROCKWORTH, *Coopers Hill and Stroud Road c1955* B837009

There is still a petrol station on this site at Brockworth roundabout, though the wartime Nissen hut we see here is long gone. The backdrop to this scene is Coopers Hill, where each Whit Monday the famous cheese-rolling event takes place. This continues a bizarre, centuries-old tradition, in which participants race down a precipitous slope in pursuit of a Double Gloucester cheese.

BROCKWORTH
From Castle Hill c1955
B837006

The Gloster Aircraft factory can be seen in the middle distance. The firm was founded in Cheltenham, but moved to this site in the 1920s. Many historic aircraft, such as the Gloster Gladiator, the Hawker Hurricane and the Gloster Meteor were built on this site. It was also here that the E28/39, Britain's first jet aeroplane, was produced in the early 1940s.

BROCKWORTH, *Ermin Street c1960* B837030

When this photograph of the Gloster Aircraft Company complex was taken, aircraft production was drawing to a close. The firm's final product, a delta-winged Gloster Javelin, took off from the factory's airstrip in 1963. British Nylon Spinners took over the site, followed by ICI Fibres, then Du Pont.

BROCKWORTH
The Church and Brockworth Court c1960 B837002

Today, Brockworth is altogether urbanised, a suburb of Gloucester. But when this photograph was taken, it was a village with its own character and community. The tranquil scene captured here reminds us how large-scale housing development in the past few decades has changed the nature of so many former villages. Brockworth church is late Norman and 13th-century, while the adjacent Brockworth Court dates from the 16th century and was built for the last prior of Llanthony.

▶ **BARNWOOD**
*Barnwood Road
c1955* B529005

Barnwood stands on Ermin Street, which was built by the Romans to link the two important towns of Glevum (Gloucester) and Corinium (Cirencester), so the road we see in this picture has been in use for 2,000 years. The two pairs of houses nearest the camera on the left were demolished in 1964 when the dual carriageway was built.

◀ **BARNWOOD**
The Church c1960
B529006

Barnwood is mentioned in the Domesday Book, at which time it was owned by St Peter's Abbey in Gloucester. The church is Norman in origin with later additions, including the 15th-century tower.

▲ **HUCCLECOTE,** *The View from Birdlip Hill c1960* H337012

While staying in Gloucestershire in 1863, Lewis Carroll described the view across the Severn Vale as 'marked out just like a giant chessboard'. This, it is said, gave him the idea for the chessboard scenes and characters in his classic children's fantasy *Alice through the Looking-Glass*. As we look at this view from Birdlip across the Vale to the Malverns, the Severn Estuary and the Brecon beacons beyond, it is easy to understand how the county's landscape influenced the writer

◄**HARTPURY**
St Mary's Church and the Tithe Barn c1960 H495001

The magnificent tithe barn that stands close by the church of St Mary the Virgin dates from the 15th century, and is reckoned to be the second oldest in the country. Grade II listed, the stone-built barn measures 162ft long by 36ft wide, and is still in use to this day. At the time this photograph was taken the building was roofed with slates, but these were replaced by red tiles during restorations in 1981.

AROUND CHELTENHAM

CHELTENHAM

The Centre and the Promenade c1955 C75007

Today this area of Cheltenham is pedestrianised, but back in the 1950s traffic negotiated the ornamental roundabout. The department store Shirer & Lance's was founded in the 1830s, and occupied most of the Colonnade. It ceased trading in 1979, but it is remembered by many. Midway along the range of buildings on the left we can see the 'Coal' sign which stood above Riches' shop. Though tiny, Riches was an emporium for children, because besides anthracite and nutty slack it boasted the best collection of Dinky Toys in town.

▼ **CHELTENHAM,** *The Promenade c1960* C75154

Once eulogised in The Times as 'the most beautiful thoroughfare in Britain', Cheltenham's Promenade began its existence as a walkway from the High Street to a spa pump room that stood where the Queen's Hotel now stands. Apart from its pedestrianisation, much of the Promenade is unchanged since this photograph was taken.

▶ **CHELTENHAM**
High Street c1950 C75032

The imposing building in the left foreground is home to Lloyd's Bank; it replaced the town's Assembly Rooms in 1900. A little further down, The Plough Hotel, an ancient coaching inn, was demolished to make way for the Regent Arcade shopping mall, which was officially opened by the Princess Royal in 1985.

◀ **CHELTENHAM**
Lower High Street
c1955 C75109

The turreted building in the distance is the boys' grammar school, which was demolished in the mid 1960s. This is the original part of Cheltenham, pre-dating the grander areas that grew up when the town rose to prominence as a fashionable spa. Some of the buildings here are much older than their early Victorian facades suggest. Then as now, though, the Lower High Street is a bustling place of small shops and independent businesses.

▶ **CHELTENHAM**
St Paul's Hospital
c1965 C75130

Thousands of Cheltenham people entered the world at St Paul's maternity hospital in Swindon Road, which was founded in 1948. Less happily, the site was originally the town's workhouse, but large-scale redevelopment in the 1990s swept away the reminder of those days of hardship.

◄ **CHARLTON KINGS**
Charlton Hill from Cirencester Road c1955
C445002

Before World War II, a by-pass was planned for Cheltenham. Bradley Road, which we see here, was the only section completed before local objections and the outbreak of hostilities shelved the plan indefinitely. Until the 1960s, Charlton Kings railway station stood half a mile up the hill from this spot - its site is now an industrial park. Another change is The New Inn, since renamed The Little Owl after a Gold Cup winning racehorse.

◀ CHARLTON KINGS
Cirencester Road
c1955 C445003

These bay-windowed houses in Cirencester Road were built in the 1930s to meet the needs of Cheltenham's growing population. They were built of concrete blocks by the Swindon development company Bradleys on land that was formerly Fuller & Maylam's nursery.

▲ **PRESTBURY,** *Deep Street c1960* P112019

Cheltenham's famous racecourse is named Prestbury Park after the village that is situated at its outskirts. Prestbury was home to Fred Archer, the most celebrated jockey of his age. During his short career Archer notched up 2148 wins from 8004 mounts, but despite this success he took his own life while in a state of temporary insanity induced by typhoid fever, according to the coroner's verdict.

◀ CLEEVE HILL
The Rising Sun Hotel
c1960 C115045

Glorious views across the Severn Vale to the Malvern Hills add to the charms of The Rising Sun, which has long been a favourite watering hole for the racing fraternity. Just a short trot from here is a stone memorial at the spot where jockey George Stevens, who in Victorian times won the Grand National five times, died after falling from a horse he was riding to his home on Cleeve Hill.

CLEEVE HILL
The Racing Stables and the Old Golf Course c1955 C115018

When this photograph was taken, three leading Prestbury stables exercised their horses daily on Cleeve Hill Common. Tim Hamey's stable in Park Street, Frenchie Nicholson's in Lake Street and John Roberts in Mill Street all produced plenty of winners. But the Mill Street stable, which employed around 20 lads, had the distinction of training Four Ten, which won the Cheltenham Gold Cup in 1954.

BIRDLIP, *The View from Birdlip Hill c1955* B99010

This view looks across to Crickley Hill, which is now designated a country park. Crickley is an important archeological site, where an extensive Iron Age promontory hill fort has been under excavation since the 1960s. The honey-coloured limestone characteristic of the Cotswolds has been quarried from this area for centuries.

BIRDLIP HILL
c1955 B99011

A very different scene presents itself today as you drive along the A417 over Birdlip Hill. It now carries a huge volume of traffic to and from the M4 in one direction and the M5 in the other. This photograph is a pleasant reminder of how things once were. Incidentally, the ovoid shape of the caravan suggests that it was made by Cheltenham Caravans at the firm's Leckhampton works.

BIRDLIP, *The Royal George Hotel c1955* B99001

The Royal George is still very much in business today. A few decades ago, before universal car ownership, the Black & White coach company organised evening jaunts from its station in St Margaret's Road, Cheltenham to this popular hilltop hostelry. Excursionists had time to enjoy a swift half in the hotel's pleasure gardens before boarding the bus once more for home.

▶ **CRANHAM**
The Village c1965
C179060

Cranham has not suffered too much at the hands of unsympathetic development over the years, partly because it is situated in a steep valley and surrounded by dense woodland. The village is known far and wide to Brownies, Cubs, Guides and Scouts, because the Scouts' Association has had a fieldcraft and camp site here for many years.

◀ **CRANHAM**
c1960 C179053

Ancient woods, common land and rural lanes around unspoilt Cranham make the village a favourite with walkers. The surroundings change with the seasons, most spectacularly perhaps in autumn sunshine, when the deciduous trees glow gold, red and yellow.

▲ **CRANHAM,** *Prinknash Abbey, the Bells c1960* C179030

The oldest part of Prinknash Abbey dates from the 14th century – it was a grange of the abbots of Gloucester; the present Benedictine community arrived here from Caldey Island in 1928.

◄**CRANHAM**
Prinknash Abbey, the Foundations of the New Abbey c1960 C179016

The foundations of the new monastic building are well under way in this photograph. When it was completed in the 1960s, the uncompromisingly modern abbey was at the centre of controversy: it was hailed by some as a fine example of functional architecture, and criticised by others as stark and featureless. Perhaps easier on the eye is the pottery for which Prinknash is well known.

COLESBOURNE, *The River Churn c1960* C453014

At Colesbourne the River Churn is joined by Hilcot Brook, one of the tributaries that swell this normally slow-flowing waterway on its meandering way to Cirencester.

COLESBOURNE
c1960 C453007

Colesbourne, like its neighbouring villages of Coberley and Cowley, lies in the valley of the River Churn surrounded by the chequerwork fields that are typical of this part of Gloucestershire. In spring the millions of snowdrops that carpet the woodland around Colesbourne Park attract visitors galore.

LEIGH, *Cyder Press Farm c1955* L344005

The tiny hamlet of Leigh lies on the east bank of the River Severn, perched on land just high enough to raise it from the floodplain, a few miles north-west of Cheltenham. Although this half-timbered building is called Cyder Press Farm to this day, the great stones in the foreground are actually those of a cider mill. In days gone by village communities worked together come September time to collect apples for cider making and pears for perry.

EAST GLOUCESTERSHIRE

CIRENCESTER, *Cricklade Street c1955* C106052

Facing us in the distance is Barnett's the fishmonger's, a local business in the Market Place of long standing - it closed in 2000. F W Woolworth's on the right was built on the site of a wholesale ironmongery business founded in the 19th century by Henry Alexander, who also owned a foundry in Cricklade Street. A teetotaller, Mr Alexander opened a temperance working men's club at the premises in 1867.

CIRENCESTER, *St John's Church and Blackjack Street c1955* C106033

Owing to inadequate foundations, the tower of St John's showed signs of stress shortly after it was built in 1420. The spur buttresses that were added as an emergency measure on the north and south sides can clearly be seen in this view. Daniel George Bingham, a great benefactor to Cirencester, was born in Blackjack Street in 1830.

CIRENCESTER
Gloucester Street c1955 C106017

To the right, the cottages with overhanging upper storeys or jetties date from the 15th century. The cut stones at the front on which they rest are said to have come from the Abbey, which was demolished around 1540. The Cotswold tile-roofed house beyond this venerable pair no longer stands, and The Loyal Volunteer pub beyond it is now a private house. Back in the 18th century, however, it was a theatre, and it is said that Sarah Siddons – the darling of her day - trod the boards here. Another pub in the picture, The White Lion (left), is still open for business, although The Red Lion in the distance called last orders for the final time some while ago.

CIRENCESTER, *Tetbury Road c1955* C106025

The photographer who took this picture was positioned at the entrance to Cirencester railway station. Dr Beeching axed the line in 1964, although the tall, slim station building can be seen to this day. Said to be the work of I K Brunel, it is a fine example of Great Western Railway Victorian Gothic architecture.

▶ CIRENCESTER
The Church and the Town Hall c1955
C106022

St John's is one of the largest parish churches in the country, so it is fitting that it boasts one of the grandest entrances. Dating from the late 15th century, the three-storey porch originally housed the administrative offices for the abbey. After the Dissolution, the building became Cirencester's Town Hall, the name by which it is known to this day.

▼ CIRENCESTER
Town Approach c1955 C106006

On the small traffic island in the left foreground is the Jubilee lamp, which was paid for by public subscription to commemorate the Silver Jubilee of George V. When alterations to the junction were made, the lamp was moved to its present site in Dyer Street.

▶ CIRENCESTER
Market Place c1955
C106015

Cirencester is the quintessential English market town, and it has managed by luck and design to keep the worst ravages of modern development at bay. Each Monday and Friday a colourful street market is staged in this setting under the watchful presence of St John the Baptist's church. One of the oldest in the country, the market is mentioned in the Domesday Book.

◄ **CIRENCESTER**
The Church and Cirencester House c1955 C106012

Cirencester House has been home to the Earls of Bathurst for over two centuries; the building was designed by the first Earl. Few would claim it to be an architectural triumph, but the first Earl made a better job of landscaping the surrounding park, assisted by his friend the poet Alexander Pope.

CIRENCESTER
Cricklade Street c1960
C106117

One of the town's main shopping areas, Cricklade Street is also home to the Brewery Arts Centre, which opened in 1979. Besides a thriving complex of craft workshops and a large exhibition space, the centre also provides an entertainment venue that attracts internationally regarded performers and thousands of visitors each year.

BOURTON ON THE WATER
By the Windrush c1955
B392065

The River Windrush threads through Bourton, carpeted on either bank by broad greens. One of the village's more eccentric traditions is a football match which locals play each August Bank Holiday as they have done for many years past - up to their knees in the river. It is quite a spectacle, and crowds gather annually to witness the madness. At least they know there is no chance of the match being cancelled owing to a waterlogged pitch.

▶ **BOURTON ON THE WATER**
The Village c1955
B392064

Five bridges step over the Windrush in Bourton before it flows on downstream to the village that bears its name, and then to Barrington, Burford and Witney to join the Thames. Coronation Bridge, the most recently built, commemorates the coronation of Queen Elizabeth II in 1953. The oldest dates from 1754 and stands in front of the old Corn Mill, which opened in 1978 as the Cotswold Motor Museum.

◀ **BOURTON ON THE WATER**
The River c1955 B392069

According to the guide-book of your choice, Bourton is billed 'Queen of the Cotswolds', 'the Venice of the Cotswolds', or 'the jewel in the Cotswolds' crown'. Among its attractions are many fine country houses and cottages built from locally quarried stone that has mellowed to the colour of honey on butter. They lend a timeless charm, though few of the buildings date back further than the 17th century.

▲ **NORTHLEACH,** *The Stocks c1955* N125006

The stocks and pillory in Market Square remind us of a time when justice was swift and direct. Northleach stands on the road from South Wales to London; it became an important coaching town, where inns such as the half-timbered Kings Head we see here provided shelter and accommodation to travellers.

◀ **NORTHLEACH**
The Church c1960 N125025

The magnificent 15th-century church is dedicated to St Peter and St Paul. It was funded by local merchants grown wealthy in the wool trade, and some of their stories are told in the notable collection of brasses found inside. Along with other Cotswold wool churches in Burford, Cirencester, Fairford and Winchcombe, St Peter and St Paul's is one of the finest ecclesiastical buildings in the Perpendicular style to be seen in the country.

▼ **NORTHLEACH,** *High Street c1960* N125036

Although this scene looks tranquil, Northleach High Street was chock-a-block every day with heavy traffic until the by-pass opened in the 1990s. Today the scene is more reminiscent of this peaceful picture from the past. Most of the buildings in the town centre are of stone, although there are a few half-timbered examples.

▶ **NORTHLEACH**
Market Square c1965 N125058

Northleach lies between Cheltenham and Burford, and most of this former wool town's buildings date from Tudor and Jacobean days. Many of them have steeply pitched roofs of Cotswold stone slates, characteristic of the region. If we look carefully, we will notice that the slates are tiny at the ridge and become progressively larger lower down. Each size slate has its own name, and terms in use in former times included duchesses, countesses, short wivetts, movedays and bachelors.

◀ **NORTHLEACH**
Market Square
c1965 N125049

The town centre has changed remarkably little in the decades since this photograph was taken. But it is curious to note that every car captured here - Ford, Vauxhall, Morris, Austin, Riley, Wolseley - was made in Britain. Such a scene would be a great rarity today.

▶ **NORTHLEACH**
Church Farm
Cottages c1955
N125004

Before agriculture became mechanised, large numbers of people were employed on the land; in Gloucestershire many of them lived in tied farm cottages such as these. In the foreground we see a millstone, possibly once used to grind corn, but more likely to crush apples for cider making.

NORTHLEACH
The Green c1955 N125008

The half-timbered houses with one storey overhanging the next look picturesque to modern eyes, but originally those jetties (as overhangs are called) served a purpose. In time, the effect of heavy furniture in upstairs rooms caused the floor joists to sag, but this was counterbalanced by extending the joists over the wall beneath and adding the weight of walls and roof to the timbers' outer edge. Jetties also served to throw rain water away from the walls, and they were a way of cheating the tax man. If you lived in such a property you paid tax on the area covered by the building at ground level, so the extra floor space upstairs was a bonus.

STOW ON THE WOLD
The Green c1955 S260044

Stow sits on the Roman Fosse Way, 800ft up on a rounded tump. The surrounding landscape was excellent sheep country, and wealthy wool merchants built themselves fine stone houses - some grand, some modest - as we see here. The Green was much larger a century ago, and old photographs show sheep grazing on it. Beneath the tree are the town stocks, which have been moved to a different part of the Green since this picture was taken. They date back to the 15th century, and originally stood in the town square.

BIBURY, *Arlington Row c1960* B530024

One of the most picturesque - and most photographed - rows of cottages in the Cotswolds, Arlington Row's first function was a barn. Then in the 17th century the building was converted into home workers' cottages for weavers in the wool trade. Traditionally, weavers' cottages had stable doors; the top half was left open so that passing traders could see the quality of the work in progress. Arlington Row is now owned by the National Trust. In the foreground is the River Coln.

BIBURY
The Swan Hotel c1960
B530026.

Bibury is a spread-out settlement because it was formed from a number of tiny hamlets and individual properties that gradually grew together over the centuries. One of its grander buildings is the Swan Hotel, which has been providing accommodation and refreshment to guests for over 200 years. William Morris called Bibury the most beautiful village in England. Many of the thousands of visitors who arrive each year drawn by the trout farm and other local attractions probably leave in agreement with him.

LOWER SLAUGHTER, *The Post Office c1955* L313009

Don't be fooled into thinking that the name of this village suggests a bloodthirsty past. Some old guide-books claim that the name derives from the sloe (or blackthorn) tree, but it more likely comes from 'slough', meaning a muddy place. The River Eye flows through the village; there has been a mill here since before the Norman Conquest, though the present building with the tall chimney shown here dates from around 1800.

LECHLADE
The Round House c1955
L147036

This Round House, like others along the man-made waterway, was lived in by a lengthman and his family - they collected tolls from passing barges on the Thames and Severn canal. Built in the latter half of the 18th century, the canal ran from Inglesham to Stroud, where it joined the Stroudwater Navigation to the River Severn at Framilode.

LECHLADE
Burford Street c1955
L147053

St Lawrence's Church was built in the Perpendicular style, and features a number of grotesque gargoyles that stare down from the eaves. The church was paid for by merchants made rich from wool. Lechlade's function as a market town was overshadowed by its near neighbour Fairford. Nevertheless, Lechlade played host to a livestock fair until the late 1950s. Here we can see some of the town's fine Georgian buildings.

FAIRFORD, *The Bridge c1960* F145021

The River Coln flows through Fairford on its way to meet the Thames just a few meandering miles on. The town has its place in the history of aviation, for on 9 April 1969 Captain Brian Trubshaw flew Concorde 002 from Filton in Bristol to RAF Fairford, which was the aircraft's flight test base for the next seven years. Fairford is also home to the annual International Air Show.

FAIRFORD
The Mill c1960 F145028

Beyond the mill, which dates from Norman times and was used for fulling cloth, is the square tower of St Mary's. This parish church was rebuilt in the 15th century; it has some fine stained glass in 28 windows paid for by John Tame, a rich wool merchant. According to local legend, the glass was captured by John Tame as it was on its way to Rome by ship. The truth is more likely to be that the windows arrived in this country by ship from Flanders, where many of them were made.

FAIRFORD, *The Market Place c1960* F145019

Besides being a market centre and wool town, Fairford was on an important coaching route in the days of horse-drawn travel, as it straddled the road from London to the south-west. Echoes of its former wealth can be seen in the fine 17th- and 18th-century stone buildings in the Market Place.

▼ **CHEDWORTH,** *The Church c1955* C446017

The late Norman church of St Andrew was greatly altered in the 15th century. To stand in the nave is like being inside a lantern as light floods in through the large Perpendicular windows. Among the church's interesting curiosities are a sundial on the south wall, a stout Norman tub font and a delicately carved 15th-century pulpit. The belfry contains six bells, all cast by Rudhall's foundry of Gloucester.

▶ **CHEDWORTH**
Upper Chedworth c1955 C446012

Chedworth is a sprawling village with Cotswold stone cottages that cling to the valley sides. In the heyday of the woollen industry, shepherds and their families came from Wales to live here and tend sheep in the surrounding countryside. Consequently the village was bi-lingual, with Welsh and English spoken in equal measure. Chedworth is famous for its well-preserved Roman villa, which was discovered in 1864 when a gamekeeper digging a ferret out of a rabbit burrow discovered fragments of mosaic. The villa has been owned by the National Trust since 1924.

◀ **SHERBORNE**
The Post Office
c1960 S762004

The Cotswold village of Sherborne lies between Northleach and Burford. It is an ancient fording point on Sherborne Brook, a tributary of the River Windrush. Many of the neat stone cottages, like the ones we see here, were lived in by workers on the Sherborne Estate. The church of St Mary Magdelene was rebuilt in 1850, but it has 14th-century origins. Inside is a memorial to John Dutton, lord of the manor, who died in 1656; it reads 'Master of a large fortune and owner of a mind equal to it.'

▶ **TARLTON**
Church Road c1955
T334001

A few miles to the south-west of Cirencester, Tarlton has Saxon origins, though they are well concealed. Brick, rather than Cotswold stone, is much in evidence here, which gives the village a more workaday character than some of its more picturesque near neighbours. The centrepiece of this scattered village is the church, rebuilt in the Norman revivalist style in 1875. The adjacent school building is also Victorian.

NORTH GLOUCESTERSHIRE

WINCHCOMBE, *North Street c1960* W378018

Winchcombe (or Winchcomb as it was spelt until the Victorians added the final 'e' for no good reason), like many of its Cotswold neighbours, was a wool town. The surrounding landscape was excellent sheep country, and Cotswold Lions were best suited to the conditions, a hardy breed with fleeces especially thick to keep out the chill and make their owners rich.

65

▶ **WINCHCOMBE**
Gloucester Street and the Church c1955 W378005

St Peter's is a splendid 15th-century church built in the Perpendicular style, although the interior was substantially renovated in 1872. The church boasts some of the most grotesque gargoyles in the Cotswolds. There are 40 of them in total, some representing demons, ghouls and ghosts, while the remainder are caricatures of people who lived hereabouts at the time when the waterspouts were carved. In the nave are two stone coffins discovered when the site of the Benedictine abbey was excavated by archaeologists in 1892. One is said to contain the remains of St Kenelm, the boy saint. The other is the coffin of King Kenulf, who ruled the Saxon kingdom of Mercia from AD796-821.

▶ **HAILES**
The Abbey c1960 H5037

The remains of Hailes (sometimes spelt Hayles) Abbey lie a mile or two out of Winchcombe off the B4632 to Broadway. Consecrated in 1252 at ceremony with a distinguished guest list that included Henry III, his wife Queen Eleanor of Provence, 300 assorted nobles and knights and fourteen bishops, Hailes Abbey was one of Gloucestershire's grandest monastic foundations.

WINCHCOMBE, *High Street c1960* W378016

Behind the wall on the left stood Winchcombe Abbey, which the people of Winchcombe were given the opportunity to buy when Henry VIII dissolved the monasteries. They declined the offer, and instead used the great church as a source of building material. Masonry, timbers, fixtures and fittings once erected to the glory of God were incorporated over the centuries into other buildings all over Winchcombe and beyond.

◄ **TEWKESBURY**
The Cross and High Street c1955 T26051

Tewkesbury's cross stands at the meeting point of the town's three main roads – the High Street, Church Street and Barton Street. The present structure was erected in 1920 as a war memorial, but a previous cross was built on the site in about 1500 to commemorate the Battle of Tewkesbury. In 1650 the original cross was unceremoniously taken down and its stones used to repair the Long Bridge.

TEWKESBURY
Church Street c1955
T26057

In the days of horse-drawn travel, Tewkesbury was an important coaching town. By 1830 some 30 stage coaches a day pulled into Tewkesbury, bringing passengers to feed and accommodate, horses to water and rest, and a great deal of business to the local community. The Hop Pole Hotel on the left in this photograph was a posting house, where horses could be changed and packages left for delivery to other towns. The most famous stagecoach was *L'Hirondelle*, which covered the 122 miles from Birkenhead Ferry to Tewkesbury in 9 hours.

TEWKESBURY, *King John's Bridge c1960* T26090

King John's bridge has straddled the Avon at Tewkesbury for some 800 years. The original early 13th-century bridge built on the orders of the monarch was of stone with a half-mile-long wooden causeway across the Ham. To ensure that the bridge was well maintained, King John declared that tolls from Tewkesbury markets on Wednesdays and Saturdays should be earmarked for its upkeep. This did not happen, however, and at the County Assizes in 1638 Tewkesbury was instructed to repair the bridge because 'diverse of his majesty's subjects travelling that way have been unfortunately drowned.' In 1824 the bridge was widened, and the structure we see today is the result of a complete rebuild in 1962.

TEWKESBURY
The River Avon c1960
T26100

Boat building in Tewkesbury dates back to at least 1401, when the town was ordered to supply a ship for Henry IV's navy. The town's leading boat builder during the 20th century was C Bathurst, whose Avon Boat Building Works occupied the site we see here. In addition to building boats, Bathursts hired them out and ran a pair of steam river cruisers - the *River Queen* and the *River King* - which were able to accommodate parties of up to 475 people.

TEWKESBURY, *Mill Bank c1960* T26121

Facing us is Abbey Mill, whose origins date back eight centuries to the time when monks from the Benedictine monastery diverted the River Avon to power the mill to grind the corn that made their daily bread. For a time in the mid 19th century the mill fell out of use, but it achieved some celebrity by featuring as Abel Fletcher's mill in the successful Victorian novel *John Halifax, Gentleman* by Mrs Craik, whose memorial can be seen in the abbey church.

▼ **TIRLEY,** *The School c1950* T223005

Tirley lies a few miles downstream from Tewkesbury on the Severn. The school was established by the church in 1842, and its design is typical of others found in villages hereabouts. A curiosity of the church is its clock, which was made just after the Great War by Hubert John Carter, the village jack-of-all-trades. Still in use today, the remarkable timepiece was built from odds and ends, including a pistol barrel, a starting handle, parts of farm machinery, a file, a spade, the remains of a beam drill, components from a penny farthing bicycle, a circular saw blade, 6in nails, a gimlet, the backplate of a baker's oven and lawn mower parts.

▶ **MORETON IN MARSH**
High Street c1960
M244025

If you are a fan of open markets, Moreton on a Tuesday is your birthday and Christmas all rolled into one! The broad High Street seethes with bargain hunters in search of, well, anything from five pounds of braising steak to 'a genuine antique Victorian commode in walnut with inlaid stringing.' It is one of the biggest markets in the country with up to 300 stalls, and for the day the town's population is doubled.

◄ **MORETON IN MARSH**
The White Hart Hotel and the Curfew Bell c1960 M244029

At one time the town was called Moreton Henmersche, and then the latter word was replaced by the equally unflattering 'in Marsh'. The description has nothing to do with the bogginess of the surrounding land, although Moreton was a fording place on the River Evenlode. Marsh was originally spelt March, a Middle English word meaning border, because the town stood on the border of Gloucestershire, Oxfordshire, Warwickshire and Worcester. The story of the curfew bell is told in the caption to photograph M244192 (page 74).

► **MORETON IN MARSH**
The Manor House Hotel c1955
M244012

Moreton was a market town for the woollen industry in centuries past, and it was also an important centre for the linen weaving industry and a coaching town in the days of horse-drawn travel. Its roots are much older, though, for it straddles the Roman Fosse Way, which cuts a course straight as a die from Cirencester through to Leicestershire. Buildings, most of them built of locally-quarried limestone, grew up along this road, and a number of former coaching inns can be seen to this day. The Manor House Hotel was built in c1545, and George VI visited during World War II.

▶ MORETON IN MARSH
The Curfew Tower
c1960 M244192

Between 1633 and 1860 a bell was tolled daily in the town's 15th-century Curfew Tower owing to an unusual bequest. Sir Robert Fry returned from London on horseback to arrive at Moreton, or somewhere near it, in a pea-souper fog. Man and horse wandered about on the common unable to find their way home, until eventually the curfew bell rang and its resounding tones led them home. In gratitude, Sir Robert left an endowment of £1 a year for the clock in the tower to be wound, and ten shillings (50p) for the curfew bell to be rung daily at 5am and 8pm in summer, and at 6am and 8pm in winter.

◀ MORETON IN MARSH
The Redesdale Hall
c1955 M244014

The clock turret of Moreton's most prominent building displays the date of its construction as 1887, and on the south wall is the coat of arms of the Redesdale family of Batsford Park who funded the hall. Moreton is an administrative centre for the North Cotswolds. Also here is the National Fire Service College, which each year hosts training courses for 7,000 senior fire officers and firefighters from the UK and all over the world.

▲ **MORETON IN MARSH,** *High Street c1965* M244043

There is a pleasing lack of uniformity about the facades and rooflines of the buildings in the High Street, some of which are small cottages, and others grand town houses. In the 17th century the building that is now The White Hart Royal was a manor house, and Charles I stayed there in July 1644 after the Battle of Marston Moor. He probably was not in the best of spirits, as his army had just lost 4,000 men and had another 1,500 captured.

◄ **CHIPPING CAMPDEN**
Church Cottages c1955
C335037

Presiding over the town is the 120ft high pinnacle-topped tower of St James', which dates from the 15th century. In the churchyard, a tombstone to Marther Hiron who died in 1708 bears the verse: 'Here lieth a virgin pure and chaste, Who did not want her time to waste. She dearly longed to married be, To Christ her Lord and none but he. And now she has her soul at rest, With glorious sounds for ever blest.'

▼ **CHIPPING CAMPDEN,** *The Church c1960* C335042

'Chipping' means 'market' in Old English, and it was as a market centre for the woollen industry that Chipping Campden rose to affluence. The town boasts many fine stone buildings, including the early 17th-century almshouses we see in the foreground here and St James' Church - one of the most magnificent in the Cotswolds - beyond.

▶ **CHIPPING CAMPDEN**
High Street c1960 C335047

Here we glimpse the High Street through the arches of the Market Hall, which was built in 1627 at the expense of Sir Baptist Hicks. This rich London merchant won favour with James I by lending the monarch money, and in return he was granted 'our rectory and church at Cheltenham, our chapel at Charlton Kings and our church at Campden.'

◄ **CHIPPING CAMPDEN**
High Street c1955
C335032

Chipping Campden is a centre of fine craftsmanship to this day; this is a legacy of the architect Charles Ashbee, who in 1902 brought 100 silversmiths, furniture makers and other craftsmen with their families from London's East End to establish the Guild of Handicraft in the town.

► **CHIPPING CAMPDEN**
High Street c1955
C335024

Thanks to restoration work by the Campden Trust, this honey-hued stone town has some of the finest buildings in the county. Just beyond the Market Hall behind the war memorial is the Town Hall, which dates back to the 14th century. Other fine examples in the High Street include the 18th-century Bedfont House, the 14th-century Woolstaplers Hall and the early 19th-century Lygon Arms.

▶ MICKLETON
Main Street c1960
M250010a

A few miles to the north of Chipping Campden lies Mickleton, a small town that displays both the limestone buildings of the Cotswolds and the traditional half-timbered style of the Vale. The Morris 1000 is heading west past the post office towards Tudor House - with its steeply pitched roof of stone tiles, it is one of Mickleton's notable buildings.

◀ STANTON
The Village c1960 S501005

It is no surprise that Stanton features on chocolate box lids, as it is everyone's idea of how a Cotswold village should look. Today many of the cottages are holiday homes, and consequently Stanton can feel as though the door has been locked while the inhabitants are away. Life does ebb and flow though, thanks to a pub called The Mount, which has fine views from its raised position at the other end of the village.

SOUTH GLOUCESTERSHIRE

STROUD, *The Town Centre c1965* S224090

The camera is looking towards Russell Street and George Street, with Sims clock at their junction. Before the clock was built in the early 1920s, this was the main taxi rank in the town centre. Stroud lies at the convergence of five valleys, so there is very little flat ground. Viewed from the foot of the valleys, the town appears to be built on a series of terraces, which adds to its attraction.

▶ **RODBOROUGH**
The Village c1960
R311006

The Prince Albert is a popular hostelry to this day, although Stroud Brewery - which owned the pub when this picture was taken - disappeared a good few years ago. Rodborough parish extends from Stroud to Minchinhampton on the south side of the Frome valley, and includes the hamlets of Butterrow, Houndscroft and Rodborough Common.

◀ **RODBOROUGH**
The Bear Inn c1960
R311001

Architecturally The Bear is an odd blend, part rural Cotswold, part Bavarian hunting lodge. But it is an interesting combination, and views from the inn from its position at the top of Rodborough Common are a delight. The 240-acre common is now in the care of the National Trust. The inn has changed remarkably little since this photograph was taken, although the petrol pumps are no more.

▲ **WOODCHESTER** *c1955* W130001

Lying between Stroud and Nailsworth, the parish includes the villages of North and South Woodchester. One of the best Roman mosaic pavements in the country was discovered under the parish churchyard. In the fourth century, an extensive villa of 60 rooms occupied the spot.

◀ **NAILSWORTH**
A View of the Town c1955
N1014

The A46 from Bath can be seen snaking down into Nailsworth, which lies at the meeting place of three steep and wooded valleys. Describing the town in 1826, William Cobbett wrote: 'Here are a series of spots every one of which a lover of landscapes would like to have painted. Even the buildings of the factories are not ugly.' Water power was used to drive woollen mills well into the 19th century. Today, many of the former mills have been put to other uses as industrial units or as retail outlets.

NAILSWORTH
Bridge Street c1955
N1004

If we look carefully, we will see five bicycles in this photograph, which suggests that the people of Nailsworth were as fit as fleas in the 1950s. Bridge Street, like all others in the town, leads down to the Cross. So wherever those cyclists were going, they had a steep climb one way or the other.

PAINSWICK *c1965* P3031

Four miles from Stroud, picturesque Painswick titles itself 'Queen of the Cotswolds'. At the heart of the village is the churchyard with its 99 yew trees; surrounding it are stone houses, shops and hotels, some steeply gabled and half-timbered, others Georgian with elegant facades. Above the town, rising to 900ft, is Painswick Beacon with its golf course and ancient British hill fort.

PAINSWICK, *St Mary's Church c1965* P3025

The church was built between 1377 and 1399. Its tower houses an impressive peal of 12 bells, and in the nave are an ornamented Tudor tomb and a 17th-century font. At the annual Clipping ceremony, parishioners hold hands and form a ring round the church while singing hymns, continuing a local tradition that is centuries old.

▶ **STONEHOUSE**
High Street c1955
S265010

Standing in the Severn Vale to the west of Stroud, Stonehouse was once a cloth-making town. This activity is all but gone today, although Stonehouse remains a working town in character. It has a thriving local economy, and the modern Elgin Mall shopping centre and new housing estates have grown up in recent decades.

◀ **DURSLEY**
Market Place c1960
D72085

Owing to an unfortunate one-way traffic system foisted on the town since this photograph was taken, Dursley's Market House and Town Hall is now isolated on a roundabout. The building dates from 1738, and at one time the local cheese and butter market was held here. A little way out of town on the splendidly named Nibley Knoll is a soaring monument to William Tyndale, who translated the New Testament into English.

▲ **DURSLEY,** *The Church c1955* D72029

The tower of the parish church was rebuilt in 1709. According to the Rev Kilvert's diary of 1873, couples on their way to evening services in winter followed a practical though unusual local tradition: 'My Mother says that at Dursley, when ladies and gentlemen went out together on dark nights, the gentlemen pulled out the tails of their shirts and walked before to show the way. These were called Dursley lanterns.'

◀ **DURSLEY**
Long Street c1960 D72058

Though originally a market town, Dursley has long benefited from the presence of local industries making such things as agricultural machinery, diesel engines and furniture. Chief engineer at the well-known Dursley firm of Lister's in the 1890s was Mikael Pedersen. Cyclists have much to thank this Dane for, as he invented the Dursley-Pedersen bike. Before this there had been penny farthings, hobby horses, bikes with wooden frames and all manner of machines. But Pedersen's design was the grandfather of the modern cycle as we know it.

▶ **DURSLEY**
*Parsonage Street
c1960* D72068

This bustling scene captures the essence of many small towns in the 1960s before the arrival of multiple retailers introduced a uniformity to almost every shopping street everywhere. The shop on the right with the sunshade is Hillier's Bacon Curing Company, a firm founded in 1819 by Isaac Hillier in a former Nailsworth woollen mill.

◀ **DURSLEY**
The Post Office c1950
D72012

Built in the inter-war years, the post office is typical of many similar government and public administration buildings of the time that can be seen around the country. It is possible that the novelist Evelyn Waugh sometimes bought his stamps here, as he lived at nearby Stinchcombe.

▲ **CAM,** *Chapel Street c1955* C11003

Above The Forester's Arms' door is a sign for Cheltenham Ales, which is a brand name with a long lineage. The Cheltenham Original Brewery took over Gardner's Brewery in 1888, and in 1897 it swallowed up the rival Cheltenham Steam Brewery. Over the next three decades it bought out other brewers in Nailsworth, Stow-on-the-Wold, Northleach, Gloucester, Wickwar and Evesham. Then in 1945 the Hereford & Tredegar Brewery was acquired, and the name changed to Cheltenham & Hereford Breweries Ltd; in 1959 it merged with Stroud Brewery. Whitbread's acquired this business in 1966.

◀ **ULEY**
From Uley Bury c1965
U3029

Uley Brewery is in business to this day, one of a number of small breweries in the area that produce highly distinctive beers. The firm's products can be sampled in local pubs, some of which are good examples of 18th-century architecture - The King's Head, for example, with its brightly painted sign that dates from the time of George I.

ULEY
The Street c1965 U3019

Uley rose to prosperity as a cloth-making centre, but when the Industrial Revolution shifted production from weavers' cottages to industrial factories, Uley's fortunes went into decline. Housing developments in recent decades and the nearby M5 motorway today make Uley a popular place to live for people who work in Gloucester or Bristol, but want a country address.

TETBURY, *Long Street c1965* T155072

Most of Tetbury's town centre buildings have stood there since Queen Elizabeth I's time. The Market House is one of the finest in Gloucestershire, and dates from 1655. It stands on arcades supported on chubby stone legs; beneath it is a tank from which water was pumped for public use, a benefaction to the townspeople that was installed in 1749 by Vicar Wight at his own expense. A general market is still held in and under the Market Hall on Wednesdays.

TETBURY
From Bath Bridge c1955
T155049

At first sight, Bath Bridge seems an unnecessarily grand structure to cross the tiny stream that flows beneath. This is because when the road to Bath became a turnpike in the 1770s, the Turnpike Commissioners engaged a local stonemason named Thomas Webb to build a ramp into the town that would ease the steep gradient. That is the purpose that Bath Bridge was designed to serve - the fact that it crosses a small tributary of the Avon is incidental.

BERKELEY, *Market Place c1960* B72058

The Vale of Berkeley has long been a rich agricultural area. In days gone by, Berkeley cheese was as famous as Double Gloucester, and in recent times this locally-made delicacy has enjoyed a revival in popularity. Almost equidistant from Gloucester and Bristol, situated on the southern side of the Severn Estuary, Berkeley is a small market town, a trading centre for the surrounding rural community, as it has been for centuries.

▼ **BERKELEY,** *High Street c1960* B72028

The arched entrance to The White Hart (centre) reminds us that this inn, along with others in the town such as The Berkeley Arms, rang to the clatter of hooves in the days of horse-drawn coaches. But Berkeley's importance in former times goes back much further. In Saxon days this was a borough in its own right, and a Royal Mint was located in the town.

▶ **BERKELEY**
The Square c1955 B72042

The substantial stone buildings to be seen in the town here in the Square and also around Salter Street hint at the wealth made by local merchants, who made their money in trade and shipping. Well into the 19th century, ships of up to 40 tons moored in the harbour area, bringing such commodities as salt, fruit, pottery, lead and timber.

BERKELEY
The Old House c1955
B72009

The rickety-looking oriel window on its timber props and horned sash window frames are Victorian additions to the centuries-old corner house, which was a shop at the time this photograph was taken. But without doubt the most venerable building hereabouts is Berkeley Castle, the oldest inhabited in England. Berkeley Castle gained notoriety in 1327 when Edward II was murdered within its walls. The oubliette - a deep and uncomfortable pit into which the unfortunate monarch was cast - can be seen to this day. Incidentally, it was in the castle that Dickie Pearce, England's last court jester, died while midway through a performance.

BERKELEY
High Street 1956 B72026

Delightfully neat and compact in appearance, the buildings that jostle shoulder to shoulder along the street are deceptively older than they look. Many were given a fashionable facelift in Victorian times with additions such as the bay fronts to the cottages on the right. But behind the facades are centuries-old houses, some of them timber-framed.

▼ **SHARPNESS,** *The Docks c1955* S502011

Timber is being loaded onto barges, or lighters, to be towed up to Gloucester, where vast wood yards were sited along the canal. The wood came from Scandinavia, Russia and Canada, and was used in the city's furniture and match-making industries. Many local people will remember that 'England's Glory' matches were made in Gloucester at the Bristol Road factory of S J Moreland & Sons. Other cargoes that were taken by barge from Sharpness to Gloucester included salt, oil, chocolate, wheat and copper. However, from the mid 1960s canal traffic dwindled in the face of competition from road transport.

▶ **SHARPNESS**

The Training Ship 'Vindicatrix'
c1955 S502018

Lighters, such as the ones we see moored here in the foreground, were the workhorses on the Gloucester to Sharpness canal, which when it opened in 1827 was the longest in Britain. Nearby is the training ship *Vindicatrix*, but larger vessels with a carrying capacity of up to 1,200 tons could negotiate the waterway. Perhaps the most unusual ships to ply the 16 miles from the Severn Estuary to Britain's most inland port were two Royal Navy submarines that arrived in Gloucester as part of a recruitment drive in 1937.

SHARPNESS
The Severn Railway Bridge c1955 S502006

When it opened in October 1879, the Severn Railway Bridge was hailed as wonder of engineering. Vessels collided with the bridge quite frequently, but the fatal blow came in October 1960. Two oil tankers, the *Arkendale H* and the *Wastdale H*, collided in fog and smashed into the bridge. Then less than two years later another oil tanker hit the bridge, to be followed by two floating cranes that inflicted more damage. This Severn landmark was dismantled in 1967, but a number of the spans were shipped intact to Chile, where they are in use today as a road bridge.

BEACHLEY
The Severn Bridge c1960 B38038

The £8 million suspension bridge was opened by Queen Elizabeth II in September 1966 to carry the new M4 motorway from England across the Severn Estuary to South Wales. Also at the ceremony were Prince Philip, the Duke of Beaufort, the Archbishop of Wales, the Secretary of State for Wales and the Bishop of Bristol.

THE FOREST OF DEAN

LYDNEY, *The Harbour c1960* L200039

In 1810 the Severn & Wye Railway Company developed Lydney Harbour, constructing the canal, dock basin and lock gates we see in the photograph. The town became a thriving port, from which 200 vessels a year carried 265,000 tons of Forest of Dean coal. When mining declined in the 20th century, Lydney's role as a port declined too, and it closed in about 1950. Now Lydney's industrial estate is situated in this area, although one commercial vessel - the MV *Balmoral* - still uses the port to carry pleasure passengers along the estuary in summer.

LYDNEY
High Street c1955
L200012

There are not many ancient buildings in the centre of Lydney, but Nos 6 and 7 the High Street are worth a special look. Dating from the 16th century, these were once the town's manor house.

LYDNEY, *Newerne Street c1955* L200011

Newerne Street is Lydney's main shopping area; it has undergone a great deal of redevelopment since this photograph was taken. The Austin van facing the camera on the left is parked outside the old Red & White coach station, and no doubt local people of ripening years will recall family holidays that began and ended at this spot.

LYDNEY
Newerne Street 1950 L200009

Depending on which dictionary of place names you read, the name Lydney means either 'water meadow', or 'sailor's island'. Either interpretation suggests that the town was once closer to the Severn than it is today - and that is the case. When the town was granted its market charter in 1268, the west bank of the Severn lay close to St Mary's parish church, and a tidal inlet called Lydney Pill extended inland as far as the High Street. The area we see here around Newerne Street would have then been under water, or at least permanently marshy.

NEWENT, *Broad Street c1955* N180033

The main shopping areas of Broad Street and Church Street have not changed too much in character since the camera clicked on this scene. Now as then, most of the shops in town are run by independent traders, so the worst excesses of corporate retail fascias have been avoided. Newent has been a market town since Henry III granted it a charter in the 13th century, and it is appropriate that the Market House, which stands on stilts and is some four centuries old, is located at the heart of the town.

NEWENT
Broad Street c1965
N180064

Newent is best enjoyed on foot. With such an assortment of architectural styles in the town centre, there is always a building or detail to please the eye. This photograph looks towards Church Street. On the right is the elegant Georgian frontage of Lloyd's Bank, complete with a fanlight over the door and a decorated gable at the roofline. This is pre-dated by the white building with jetties directly ahead on the corner - beneath the render it is almost certainly half-timbered. And just two doors away is the International Stores in premises that when this picture was taken were newly built.

▶ **NEWENT**
Church Street c1965
N180052

One of Newent's present day tourist attractions is the Shambles, a museum of Victorian life that has its entrance in Church Street, a little way up on the left in this picture. Further up on the same side is St Mary's church, built in the 13th century; it was then largely rebuilt four centuries later because the nave collapsed. Just three years after this photograph was taken, the octagonal spire was found to be dangerous and was lowered.

◀ **NEWENT**
Culvert Street c1955 N180013

The town is fortunate to have retained so many old and attractive buildings, such as this range of half-timbered cottages that greets those who arrive from the direction of Gloucester to this day. It looks as though the cottages had recently been re-roofed when this picture was taken, although the animated little girl appears to be telling her seated friend about something far more interesting.

▲ **COLEFORD,** *The Speech House c1955* C315023

Midway between Coleford and Cinderford, the Speech House was built in 1676 as the Court of Verderers and Freeminers - the place where legal grievances relating specifically to the laws and customs of the Forest of Dean were aired. It was also the centre for administration of Forest business. The impressive building is now a hotel, but the ancient court room with its oak dais is preserved, and the Forest Verderers still sit there when transacting their affairs.

◄ **COLEFORD**
The View from Transport Square c1955 C315017

The isolated tower that stands in the middle of the Town Square was once attached to the parish church, which was built on the site of Coleford's old Market House in 1821. When St John's was built in 1880, the nave of the former parish church was demolished. After World War I, Coleford's unusual centrepiece was dedicated to the memory of a local war hero named Angus Buchanan VC.

▼ **COLEFORD,** *The Town Centre c1950* C315019

The black and white signpost in the foreground will bring back nostalgic memories for some of motoring as it was half a century ago. One arm of the signpost points to Gloucester, which lies on the Severn, while the other arm points to the Wye valley. In between these two great rivers lies the Forest of Dean, of which Coleford is one of the principal towns.

► **COLEFORD**
High Street c1955 C315040

The war memorial and car park occupy land on which Coleford's Market House once stood. When the English Civil War began in 1642, Parliamentary troops were garrisoned in Coleford. This presented a problem for local people, because the nearest market was in the Royalist stronghold of Monmouth. To solve the difficulty, the Parliamentary commander Colonel Berrowe established a market in Coleford. The original Market House was erected, destroyed soon after, and then rebuilt in 1661. Being a market town greatly enhanced Coleford's prosperity and status.

◄ COLEFORD
*The Town Centre
1950* C315033

The names over the shops - Ivor Griffiths and Williams the tobacconist's, Charles Kay and Birt's Stores - remind us that the Forest of Dean lies between Wales and England, embracing elements of both to create a character that is all its own. Remote though it must have been in times gone by, Coleford has been a centre of habitation for at least 2,000 years. Evidence of this was provided in the 1980s when the High Nash industrial estate was being built and a large Roman temple was discovered.

► CINDERFORD
The Triangle c1955 C448016

The Triangle is at the centre of Cinderford. The war memorial lists the names of local men who lost their lives during the two world wars, many of them while serving with the county regiment, the Glosters. Today the population of Cinderford stands at around 7,500, but up until the 19th century Cinderford was no more than a tiny hamlet clustered around the building that is now The Bridge Inn on Speech House Road. When coal mining began on a commercial scale, the town's fortunes grew rapidly. This source of prosperity came to a close in the 1960s when mining was discontinued, but in more recent decades Cinderford has re-invented itself by attracting a wealth of new businesses.

NEWNHAM
The Victoria Hotel c1965
N87063

Parts of this handsome hotel date back to the mid 16th century, though the majority of the building is later. It is said to be haunted by a chambermaid who hanged herself in an attic room. At the height of Newnham's importance as a coaching town, The Victoria was one of 20 inns.

NEWNHAM, *High Street c1955* N87012

Newnham is a delightful, Severnside town today, just as it was when this scene was captured. The broad verges and continuous avenue of trees bring green, open space to the High Street and make it an attractive place to explore. Although the town does not boast many buildings of historic interest, it has a long and illustrious past. It was once the leading port on the river, and it was from Newnham that Henry II sailed with a fleet of 400 ships and 5,000 soldiers on an expedition to Ireland in 1171.

NEWNHAM, *The Clock Tower c1955* N87019

This ornamental clock tower greets visitors who enter the town along the A48 from the direction of Gloucester. It was built in 1875, and an inscribed plaque on its base explains that it was the gift of a local benefactor.

◀ **NEWNHAM**
High Street c1955 N87048

If we look closely, we will see ladders reaching up to the eaves of The George Hotel, the white building behind the clock tower. Perhaps maintenance work was being carried out on the roof. Repairs of a more drastic kind were needed at St Peter's church on the nearby Nab headland, when it collapsed along with the cliff it stood on after severe flooding in 1360. A new church was built a little further inland, which was in turn destroyed by fire in the 19th century, and so the church had to be rebuilt once more.

◄ **NEWNHAM**
High Street c1955
N87017

The charming central Green is overlooked by houses and shops, most of which were built in the late 18th and 19th centuries when local merchants invested wealth made in the maritime trade in bricks and mortar. The first greenhouse in England is said to have been made and erected in Newnham by Sir Edward Mansell, who established the country's earliest coal-fired glass-making furnace at a works to the north end of town.

▲ **BLAKENEY,** *Blakeney Street c1950* B523029

The parish church of All Saints is unusually wide, with a tiny tower and high arched windows. It was designed by Samuel Hewlett and built in about 1820 on the site of a previous church that dated from the early 18th century. An unusual interior feature is the 15th-century stoup that serves as a font. At the time this photograph was taken, the bend in the road was a notorious accident black spot: here heavily laden lorries often came to grief on the long descent down Blakeney Hill into the village.

◄ **BLAKENEY**
High Street c1950
B523028

Blakeney stands at the edge of the Forest of Dean at the point where Blackpool Brook and Soudley Brook meet. In the background we can see the surrounding wooded hills, which within living memory were popularly known as Little Switzerland.

▼ **BLAKENEY,** *The Severn Bridge Hotel c1950* B523006

In celebration of the new crossing that carried the railway over the river, the 18th-century sandstone inn we see here was renamed The Severn Bridge Hotel in 1879. Other names in Blakeney refer to iron making, which was a thriving industry in these parts. Furnace Bottom is one example, while Pig Street is so named because pig iron was transported that way to the Severn Railway Bridge, and then by rail to Gatcombe, Bristol and beyond.

▶ **BLAKENEY**
The Severn Railway Bridge c1950 B523009

At 4,162ft from end to end, the Severn Railway Bridge was the longest bridge in England when it opened. The bridge boosted the local economy by enabling coal from the Forest of Dean to be transported across to Sharpness, from where it was shipped inland up the canal to Gloucester and the Midlands, or exported by sea via the Bristol Channel.

◀ ST BRIAVELS
Chepstow Road 1955
S710018

In the days when the Forest of Dean was a Royal hunting ground, St Briavels was its administrative center; the legacy of this former importance continues to the present time. Any man born in the Hundred of St Briavels who has worked for a year and a day in a mine within the Hundred has the right to apply to the Deputy Gaveller for 'gale', or mine working. If permission is granted he becomes a Freeminer, and can extract the mineral from that mine in return for a royalty payment to the Crown. Iron, coal, ochre and rock are worked by Freeminers in the Forest to this day.

▶ LITTLEDEAN
The Village c1955 L534015

Beyond the delivery van parked on the same side as The George Hotel stands a row of cottages once quaintly named Ship's Yud Row. The scene is recognisable today, though the National Benzole petrol station on the left has gone, and so has the long stone wall on the right. New housing estates have sprung up around the village in recent decades, but they do not seem to have driven out Littledean's famous pair of ghosts, Royalist soldiers killed in a scuffle with Parliamentarians in the Civil War. Sighting are still reported - especially after closing time.

LONGHOPE
The Village c1955 L533002

The main road (A4136) skirts Longhope, and consequently the village remains a peaceful backwater. Indeed, the scene in Church Street captured here has changed remarkably little in the past half century. The Central Stores, now owned by V A and A E Geach, is in business today and provides important service to the local community, while the house ahead with the gabled attic rooms is now the village post office.

BERRY HILL
The Post Office c1965 B849001

At the time this photograph was taken, Dennis Potter - who was born in Berry Hill on 17 May 1935 - was rising to prominence as a writer of fiction and plays. By the time of his death in 1994, Potter was established as one of the most innovative TV dramatists of his generation for works such as *Blue Remembered Hills*, which was set in the Forest of Dean, and *The Singing Detective*. The building we see here at the junction of Park Road and Coverall Road remains Berry Hill Post Office to this day, though it is now painted white and the windows have been changed. The post box set into the wall has also been replaced with one of the round variety.

CHRISTCHURCH, *The Church c1955* C447013

Occupying its peaceful spot on Ross Road, overlooking a broad green with trees, Christchurch is a modest example of the Victorian Gothic style. Since this photograph was taken the vicarage glimpsed here beyond the castellated tower has become a private house. The present incumbent lives in a modern bungalow on the plot to the other side of the church.

INDEX

Frith Book Co Titles

www.francisfrith.co.uk

The Frith Book Company publishes over 100 new titles each year. A selection of those currently available is listed below. For latest catalogue please contact Frith Book Co.

Town Books 96 pages, approximately 100 photos. **County and Themed Books** 128 pages, approximately 150 photos (unless specified). All titles hardback with laminated case and jacket, except those indicated pb (paperback)

Amersham, Chesham & Rickmansworth (pb)	1-85937-340-2	£9.99	Devon (pb)	1-85937-297-x	£9.99
Andover (pb)	1-85937-292-9	£9.99	Devon Churches (pb)	1-85937-250-3	£9.99
Aylesbury (pb)	1-85937-227-9	£9.99	Dorchester (pb)	1-85937-307-0	£9.99
Barnstaple (pb)	1-85937-300-3	£9.99	Dorset (pb)	1-85937-269-4	£9.99
Basildon Living Memories (pb)	1-85937-515-4	£9.99	Dorset Coast (pb)	1-85937-299-6	£9.99
Bath (pb)	1-85937-419-0	£9.99	Dorset Living Memories (pb)	1-85937-584-7	£9.99
Bedford (pb)	1-85937-205-8	£9.99	Down the Severn (pb)	1-85937-560-x	£9.99
Bedfordshire Living Memories	1-85937-513-8	£14.99	Down The Thames (pb)	1-85937-278-3	£9.99
Belfast (pb)	1-85937-303-8	£9.99	Down the Trent	1-85937-311-9	£14.99
Berkshire (pb)	1-85937-191-4	£9.99	East Anglia (pb)	1-85937-265-1	£9.99
Berkshire Churches	1-85937-170-1	£17.99	East Grinstead (pb)	1-85937-138-8	£9.99
Berkshire Living Memories	1-85937-332-1	£14.99	East London	1-85937-080-2	£14.99
Black Country	1-85937-497-2	£12.99	East Sussex (pb)	1-85937-606-1	£9.99
Blackpool (pb)	1-85937-393-3	£9.99	Eastbourne (pb)	1-85937-399-2	£9.99
Bognor Regis (pb)	1-85937-431-x	£9.99	Edinburgh (pb)	1-85937-193-0	£8.99
Bournemouth (pb)	1-85937-545-6	£9.99	England In The 1880s	1-85937-331-3	£17.99
Bradford (pb)	1-85937-204-x	£9.99	Essex - Second Selection	1-85937-456-5	£14.99
Bridgend (pb)	1-85937-386-0	£7.99	Essex (pb)	1-85937-270-8	£9.99
Bridgwater (pb)	1-85937-305-4	£9.99	Essex Coast	1-85937-342-9	£14.99
Bridport (pb)	1-85937-327-5	£9.99	Essex Living Memories	1-85937-490-5	£14.99
Brighton (pb)	1-85937-192-2	£8.99	Exeter	1-85937-539-1	£9.99
Bristol (pb)	1-85937-264-3	£9.99	Exmoor (pb)	1-85937-608-8	£9.99
British Life A Century Ago (pb)	1-85937-213-9	£9.99	Falmouth (pb)	1-85937-594-4	£9.99
Buckinghamshire (pb)	1-85937-200-7	£9.99	Folkestone (pb)	1-85937-124-8	£9.99
Camberley (pb)	1-85937-222-8	£9.99	Frome (pb)	1-85937-317-8	£9.99
Cambridge (pb)	1-85937-422-0	£9.99	Glamorgan	1-85937-488-3	£14.99
Cambridgeshire (pb)	1-85937-420-4	£9.99	Glasgow (pb)	1-85937-190-6	£9.99
Cambridgeshire Villages	1-85937-523-5	£14.99	Glastonbury (pb)	1-85937-338-0	£7.99
Canals And Waterways (pb)	1-85937-291-0	£9.99	Gloucester (pb)	1-85937-232-5	£9.99
Canterbury Cathedral (pb)	1-85937-179-5	£9.99	Gloucestershire (pb)	1-85937-561-8	£9.99
Cardiff (pb)	1-85937-093-4	£9.99	Great Yarmouth (pb)	1-85937-426-3	£9.99
Carmarthenshire (pb)	1-85937-604-5	£9.99	Greater Manchester (pb)	1-85937-266-x	£9.99
Chelmsford (pb)	1-85937-310-0	£9.99	Guildford (pb)	1-85937-410-7	£9.99
Cheltenham (pb)	1-85937-095-0	£9.99	Hampshire (pb)	1-85937-279-1	£9.99
Cheshire (pb)	1-85937-271-6	£9.99	Harrogate (pb)	1-85937-423-9	£9.99
Chester (pb)	1-85937-382 8	£9.99	Hastings and Bexhill (pb)	1-85937-131-0	£9.99
Chesterfield (pb)	1-85937-378-x	£9.99	Heart of Lancashire (pb)	1-85937-197-3	£9.99
Chichester (pb)	1-85937-228-7	£9.99	Helston (pb)	1-85937-214-7	£9.99
Churches of East Cornwall (pb)	1-85937-249-x	£9.99	Hereford (pb)	1-85937-175-2	£9.99
Churches of Hampshire (pb)	1-85937-207-4	£9.99	Herefordshire (pb)	1-85937-567-7	£9.99
Cinque Ports & Two Ancient Towns	1-85937-492-1	£14.99	Herefordshire Living Memories	1-85937-514-6	£14.99
Colchester (pb)	1-85937-188-4	£8.99	Hertfordshire (pb)	1-85937-247-3	£9.99
Cornwall (pb)	1-85937-229-5	£9.99	Horsham (pb)	1-85937-432-8	£9.99
Cornwall Living Memories	1-85937-248-1	£14.99	Humberside (pb)	1-85937-605-3	£9.99
Cotswolds (pb)	1-85937-230-9	£9.99	Hythe, Romney Marsh, Ashford (pb)	1-85937-256-2	£9.99
Cotswolds Living Memories	1-85937-255-4	£14.99	Ipswich (pb)	1-85937-424-7	£9.99
County Durham (pb)	1-85937-398-4	£9.99	Isle of Man (pb)	1-85937-268-6	£9.99
Croydon Living Memories (pb)	1-85937-162-0	£9.99	Isle of Wight (pb)	1-85937-429-8	£9.99
Cumbria (pb)	1-85937-621-5	£9.99	Isle of Wight Living Memories	1-85937-304-6	£14.99
Derby (pb)	1-85937-367-4	£9.99	Kent (pb)	1-85937-189-2	£9.99
Derbyshire (pb)	1-85937-196-5	£9.99	Kent Living Memories(pb)	1-85937-401-8	£9.99
Derbyshire Living Memories	1-85937-330-5	£14.99	Kings Lynn (pb)	1-85937-334-8	£9.99

Available from your local bookshop or from the publisher

Frith Book Co Titles (continued)

Lake District (pb)	1-85937-275-9	£9.99
Lancashire Living Memories	1-85937-335-6	£14.99
Lancaster, Morecambe, Heysham (pb)	1-85937-233-3	£9.99
Leeds (pb)	1-85937-202-3	£9.99
Leicester (pb)	1-85937-381-x	£9.99
Leicestershire & Rutland Living Memories	1-85937-500-6	£12.99
Leicestershire (pb)	1-85937-185-x	£9.99
Lighthouses	1-85937-257-0	£9.99
Lincoln (pb)	1-85937-380-1	£9.99
Lincolnshire (pb)	1-85937-433-6	£9.99
Liverpool and Merseyside (pb)	1-85937-234-1	£9.99
London (pb)	1-85937-183-3	£9.99
London Living Memories	1-85937-454-9	£14.99
Ludlow (pb)	1-85937-176-0	£9.99
Luton (pb)	1-85937-235-x	£9.99
Maidenhead (pb)	1-85937-339-9	£9.99
Maidstone (pb)	1-85937-391-7	£9.99
Manchester (pb)	1-85937-198-1	£9.99
Marlborough (pb)	1-85937-336-4	£9.99
Middlesex	1-85937-158-2	£14.99
Monmouthshire	1-85937-532-4	£14.99
New Forest (pb)	1-85937-390-9	£9.99
Newark (pb)	1-85937-366-6	£9.99
Newport, Wales (pb)	1-85937-258-9	£9.99
Newquay (pb)	1-85937-421-2	£9.99
Norfolk (pb)	1-85937-195-7	£9.99
Norfolk Broads	1-85937-486-7	£14.99
Norfolk Living Memories (pb)	1-85937-402-6	£9.99
North Buckinghamshire	1-85937-626-6	£14.99
North Devon Living Memories	1-85937-261-9	£14.99
North Hertfordshire	1-85937-547-2	£14.99
North London (pb)	1-85937-403-4	£9.99
North Somerset	1-85937-302-x	£14.99
North Wales (pb)	1-85937-298-8	£9.99
North Yorkshire (pb)	1-85937-236-8	£9.99
Northamptonshire Living Memories	1-85937-529-4	£14.99
Northamptonshire	1-85937-150-7	£14.99
Northumberland Tyne & Wear (pb)	1-85937-281-3	£9.99
Northumberland	1-85937-522-7	£14.99
Norwich (pb)	1-85937-194-9	£8.99
Nottingham (pb)	1-85937-324-0	£9.99
Nottinghamshire (pb)	1-85937-187-6	£9.99
Oxford (pb)	1-85937-411-5	£9.99
Oxfordshire (pb)	1-85937-430-1	£9.99
Oxfordshire Living Memories	1-85937-525-1	£14.99
Paignton (pb)	1-85937-374-7	£7.99
Peak District (pb)	1-85937-280-5	£9.99
Pembrokeshire	1-85937-262-7	£14.99
Penzance (pb)	1-85937-595-2	£9.99
Peterborough (pb)	1-85937-219-8	£9.99
Picturesque Harbours	1-85937-208-2	£14.99
Piers	1-85937-237-6	£17.99
Plymouth (pb)	1-85937-389-5	£9.99
Poole & Sandbanks (pb)	1-85937-251-1	£9.99
Preston (pb)	1-85937-212-0	£9.99
Reading (pb)	1-85937-238-4	£9.99
Redhill to Reigate (pb)	1-85937-596-0	£9.99
Ringwood (pb)	1-85937-384-4	£7.99
Romford (pb)	1-85937-319-4	£9.99
Royal Tunbridge Wells (pb)	1-85937-504-9	£9.99
Salisbury (pb)	1-85937-239-2	£9.99
Scarborough (pb)	1-85937-379-8	£9.99
Sevenoaks and Tonbridge (pb)	1-85937-392-5	£9.99
Sheffield & South Yorks (pb)	1-85937-267-8	£9.99
Sherborne (pb)	1-85937-301-1	£9.99
Shrewsbury (pb)	1-85937-325-9	£9.99
Shropshire (pb)	1-85937-326-7	£9.99
Shropshire Living Memories	1-85937-643-6	£14.99
Somerset	1-85937-153-1	£14.99
South Devon Coast	1-85937-107-8	£14.99
South Devon Living Memories (pb)	1-85937-609-6	£9.99
South East London (pb)	1-85937-263-5	£9.99
South Somerset	1-85937-318-6	£14.99
South Wales	1-85937-519-7	£14.99
Southampton (pb)	1-85937-427-1	£9.99
Southend (pb)	1-85937-313-5	£9.99
Southport (pb)	1-85937-425-5	£9.99
St Albans (pb)	1-85937-341-0	£9.99
St Ives (pb)	1-85937-415-8	£9.99
Stafford Living Memories (pb)	1-85937-503-0	£9.99
Staffordshire (pb)	1-85937-308-9	£9.99
Stourbridge (pb)	1-85937-530-8	£9.99
Stratford upon Avon (pb)	1-85937-388-7	£9.99
Suffolk (pb)	1-85937-221-x	£9.99
Suffolk Coast (pb)	1-85937-610-x	£9.99
Surrey (pb)	1-85937-240-6	£9.99
Surrey Living Memories	1-85937-328-3	£14.99
Sussex (pb)	1-85937-184-1	£9.99
Sutton (pb)	1-85937-337-2	£9.99
Swansea (pb)	1-85937-167-1	£9.99
Taunton (pb)	1-85937-314-3	£9.99
Tees Valley & Cleveland (pb)	1-85937-623-1	£9.99
Teignmouth (pb)	1-85937-370-4	£7.99
Thanet (pb)	1-85937-116-7	£9.99
Tiverton (pb)	1-85937-178-7	£9.99
Torbay (pb)	1-85937-597-9	£9.99
Truro (pb)	1-85937-598-7	£9.99
Victorian & Edwardian Dorset	1-85937-254-6	£14.99
Victorian & Edwardian Kent (pb)	1-85937-624-X	£9.99
Victorian & Edwardian Maritime Album (pb)	1-85937-622-3	£9.99
Victorian and Edwardian Sussex (pb)	1-85937-625-8	£9.99
Villages of Devon (pb)	1-85937-293-7	£9.99
Villages of Kent (pb)	1-85937-294-5	£9.99
Villages of Sussex (pb)	1-85937-295-3	£9.99
Warrington (pb)	1-85937-507-3	£9.99
Warwick (pb)	1-85937-518-9	£9.99
Warwickshire (pb)	1-85937-203-1	£9.99
Welsh Castles (pb)	1-85937-322-4	£9.99
West Midlands (pb)	1-85937-289-9	£9.99
West Sussex (pb)	1-85937-607-x	£9.99
West Yorkshire (pb)	1-85937-201-5	£9.99
Weston Super Mare (pb)	1-85937-306-2	£9.99
Weymouth (pb)	1-85937-209-0	£9.99
Wiltshire (pb)	1-85937-277-5	£9.99
Wiltshire Churches (pb)	1-85937-171-x	£9.99
Wiltshire Living Memories (pb)	1-85937-396-8	£9.99
Winchester (pb)	1-85937-428-x	£9.99
Windsor (pb)	1-85937-333-x	£9.99
Wokingham & Bracknell (pb)	1-85937-329-1	£9.99
Woodbridge (pb)	1-85937-498-0	£9.99
Worcester (pb)	1-85937-165-5	£9.99
Worcestershire Living Memories	1-85937-489-1	£14.99
Worcestershire	1-85937-152-3	£14.99
York (pb)	1-85937-199-x	£9.99
Yorkshire (pb)	1-85937-186-8	£9.99
Yorkshire Coastal Memories	1-85937-506-5	£14.99
Yorkshire Dales	1-85937-502-2	£14.99
Yorkshire Living Memories (pb)	1-85937-397-6	£9.99

See Frith books on the internet at www.francisfrith.co.uk

FRITH PRODUCTS & SERVICES

Francis Frith would doubtless be pleased to know that the pioneering publishing venture he started in 1860 still continues today. Over a hundred and forty years later, The Francis Frith Collection continues in the same innovative tradition and is now one of the foremost publishers of vintage photographs in the world. Some of the current activities include:

Interior Decoration

Today Frith's photographs can be seen framed and as giant wall murals in thousands of pubs, restaurants, hotels, banks, retail stores and other public buildings throughout the country. In every case they enhance the unique local atmosphere of the places they depict and provide reminders of gentler days in an increasingly busy and frenetic world.

Product Promotions

Frith products are used by many major companies to promote the sales of their own products or to reinforce their own history and heritage. Frith promotions have been used by Hovis bread, Courage beers, Scots Porage Oats, Colman's mustard, Cadbury's foods, Mellow Birds coffee, Dunhill pipe tobacco, Guinness, and Bulmer's Cider.

Genealogy and Family History

As the interest in family history and roots grows world-wide, more and more people are turning to Frith's photographs of Great Britain for images of the towns, villages and streets where their ancestors lived; and, of course, photographs of the churches and chapels where their ancestors were christened, married and buried are an essential part of every genealogy tree and family album.

Frith Products

All Frith photographs are available Framed or just as Mounted Prints and Posters (size 23 x 16 inches). These may be ordered from the address below. From time to time other products - Address Books, Calendars, Table Mats, etc - are available.

The Internet

Already fifty thousand Frith photographs can be viewed and purchased on the internet through the Frith websites and a myriad of partner sites.

For more detailed information on Frith companies and products, look at these sites:

www.francisfrith.co.uk
www.francisfrith.com
(for North American visitors)

See the complete list of Frith Books at:

www.francisfrith.co.uk

This web site is regularly updated with the latest list of publications from the Frith Book Company. If you wish to buy books relating to another part of the country that your local bookshop does not stock, you may purchase on-line.

For further information, trade, or author enquiries please contact us at the address below:
The Francis Frith Collection, Frith's Barn, Teffont, Salisbury, Wiltshire, England SP3 5QP.
Tel: +44 (0)1722 716 376 Fax: +44 (0)1722 716 881 Email: sales@francisfrith.co.uk

See Frith books on the internet at www.francisfrith.co.uk

FREE MOUNTED PRINT

Mounted Print
Overall size 14 x 11 inches

Fill in and cut out this voucher and return
it with your remittance for £2.25 (to cover postage and handling). Offer valid for delivery to UK addresses only.

Choose any photograph included in this book.
Your SEPIA print will be A4 in size. It will be mounted in a cream mount with a burgundy rule line (overall size 14 x 11 inches).

**Order additional Mounted Prints
at HALF PRICE (only £7.49 each*)**
If you would like to order more Frith prints from this book, possibly as gifts for friends and family, you can buy them at half price (with no additional postage and handling costs).

Have your Mounted Prints framed
For an extra £14.95 per print* you can have your mounted print(s) framed in an elegant polished wood and gilt moulding, overall size 16 x 13 inches (no additional postage and handling required).

---

* IMPORTANT!

These special prices are only available if you order at the same time as you order your free mounted print. You must use the ORIGINAL VOUCHER on this page (no copies permitted). We can only despatch to one address.

Send completed Voucher form to:
The Francis Frith Collection, Frith's Barn, Teffont, Salisbury, Wiltshire SP3 5QP

CHOOSE ANY IMAGE FROM THIS BOOK

Voucher for **FREE** and *Reduced Price Frith Prints*

Please do not photocopy this voucher. Only the original is valid, so please fill it in, cut it out and return it to us with your order.

Picture ref no	Page no	Qty	Mounted @ £7.49	Framed + £14.95	Total Cost
		1	Free of charge*	£	£
			£7.49	£	£
			£7.49	£	£
			£7.49	£	£
			£7.49	£	£
			£7.49	£	£

Please allow 28 days for delivery

* Post & handling (UK) £2.25

Total Order Cost £

Title of this book . . . .

I enclose a cheque/postal order for £ . . . .
made payable to 'The Francis Frith Collection'

OR please debit my Mastercard / Visa / Switch / Amex card
(credit cards please on all overseas orders), details below

Card Number

Issue No (Switch only)   Valid from (Amex/Switch)

Expires   Signature

Name Mr/Mrs/Ms . . . .

Address . . . .

. . . .

. . . .

. . . . Postcode . . . .

Daytime Tel No . . . .

Email . . . .

Valid to 31/12/05

Free Print – see overleaf

Would you like to find out more about Francis Frith?

We have recently recruited some entertaining speakers who are happy to visit local groups, clubs and societies to give an illustrated talk documenting Frith's travels and photographs. If you are a member of such a group and are interested in hosting a presentation, we would love to hear from you.

Our speakers bring with them a small selection of our local town and county books, together with sample prints. They are happy to take orders. A small proportion of the order value is donated to the group who have hosted the presentation. The talks are therefore an excellent way of fundraising for small groups and societies.

Can you help us with information about any of the Frith photographs in this book?

We are gradually compiling an historical record for each of the photographs in the Frith archive. It is always fascinating to find out the names of the people shown in the pictures, as well as insights into the shops, buildings and other features depicted.

If you recognize anyone in the photographs in this book, or if you have information not already included in the author's caption, do let us know. We would love to hear from you, and will try to publish it in future books or articles.

Our production team

Frith books are produced by a small dedicated team at offices in the converted Grade II listed 18th-century barn at Teffont near Salisbury, illustrated above. Most have worked with the Frith Collection for many years. All have in common one quality: they have a passion for the Frith Collection. The team is constantly expanding, but currently includes:

Jason Buck, John Buck, Douglas Mitchell-Burns, Ruth Butler, Heather Crisp, Isobel Hall, Julian Hight, Peter Horne, James Kinnear, Karen Kinnear, Tina Leary, David Marsh, Sue Molloy, Kate Rotondetto, Dean Scource, Eliza Sackett, Terence Sackett, Sandra Sampson, Adrian Sanders, Sandra Sanger, Julia Skinner, Lewis Taylor, Shelley Tolcher and Lorraine Tuck.